IMAGES
of America

BRADLEY BEACH

To my beautiful children and children-in-law and my beautiful and unique grandchildren, who continue to give me unconditional love, and to the one who is unknown to me but has always had a very special place in my heart.
—Shirley Ayres

To the ladies of my family—my wife, Dawn; daughter Amy; and mother, Shirley Jacobs—for their love, support, and even involvement in all the things I get myself into.
—Gary S. Crawford

IMAGES
of America

BRADLEY BEACH

Shirley Ayres and Gary S. Crawford

ARCADIA
PUBLISHING

Published by Arcadia Publishing
Charleston, South Carolina

Library of Congress Catalog Card Number: 2002102045

For all general information contact Arcadia Publishing at:
Telephone 843-853-2070
Fax 843-853-0044
E-Mail sales@arcadiapublishing.com

For customer service and orders:
Toll-Free 1-888-313-2665

Visit us on the Internet at www.arcadiapublishing.com

CONTENTS

ACKNOWLEDGMENTS

The following people helped write this book: Troy Bianchi, who has most of Bradley Beach's history in his house; George Moffett, who has the rest of Bradley Beach's history in his head; Reverend Mayer, Father Hillier, Rabbi Bialik, Father Gluckow, and Fani Strausser; Marion Pointsett, Bert LePree, and Rosella Capella—I miss you daily; Phyllis Quixley; Dee and Dick Johnson; Lyman Graham, who graciously shared his memories and photographs; Evelyn Stryker Lewis; Helen-Chantel Pike; Bob Stewart and Ellis Gilliam, the Asbury Park boys; Selma, David, and Norma Schechner; Ruth, Helen, and Karl Solomon; Bruce Edward Hall; Lori Torres and Ed Torres; Tom Salisbury; professional photographers Milt Edelson and Todd Robinson; Karen, Grace, and both Carols from the library; Charles Harvey, Jim Holloway Sr., and Jim Holloway Jr.; John Edison; Pat Lee; Gloria Weilandis, who generously shared her memories and photographs; Patty and Tom Rose; and members of the Bradley Beach Historical Society.

—Shirley Ayres.

Amy Lee Crawford, the 14-year-old who wrote a history of the Bradley Beach Police Department; Robert DeNardo, chief, Bradley Beach Police Department; John Gregg, retired deputy chief, Bradley Beach Police Department; Dave Johnson, president, Bradley Beach First Aid Squad; Charles W. "Rusty" King; Theresa Lee (DeVito family); North Jersey Electric Railroad Historical Society; Jo Smith Schloeder (Kirms family); William Sciarappa; Florence Kirms Smith (Kirms family); Paul and Maria Spittlehouse (Sciarappa family); Walter A. Wilson, past chief (2000), Bradley Beach Fire Department; Norman and Marie Wright; John W. Zech, chief, Bradley Beach Fire Department.

—Gary S. Crawford.

INTRODUCTION

Bradley Beach was carved out of sand dunes and pine forests by two visionaries who saw beyond the confinements of the 19th century into the 20th and 21st centuries. James A. Bradley and William B. Bradner bought property in this section of Ocean Township and started laying out building lots and streets, causing a great deal of amusement among their friends. These men, however, knew that this place would one day become a resort town, and they wanted to plan it well.

Bradley Beach today is like a New York neighborhood. Everything you need or want is right here within walking distance of your home. On Main Street, as on 46th Street, the variety of eateries makes our local "Restaurant Row" very popular. Combine dinner with a movie, and you have year-round entertainment.

Chiropractors and the 24-hour gym will shape you up and keep you coming back for more. Flowers, liquor, pastries, and jewelry—all available on Main Street—promise to keep anyone happy. Plus, there is more. Religion has a big part in our lives. What other small town with a year-round population of about 5,000 can boast of four Christian churches and two Jewish synagogues? That is not all. Bradley Beach is a pretty town. There are colorful flower beds and leafy trees up and down the streets. The tile walks on Main Street and on the boardwalk stand out from the ordinary cement walks. The big gazebo and the six smaller ones look very cozy and sheltering during the day and are tastefully lit at night. Our citizens come from various cultures and religions, adding a wonderful richness to our lives.

Now, our history needs to be preserved for future generations—not just photographs and fond memories but also historical buildings need to be saved and protected from developers. Too many beautiful old structures are leveled to build new ones, even though restoration might have brought the originals back to life. Our history is relatively new, but our children and grandchildren should be given the right to know what our town was like when William Bradner built his home and settled here with his family and James Bradley patrolled the beaches.

One

THE BIG TWO
AND TWO MORE

In 1871, William B. Bradner and his son Robert Dashell, in Ocean Grove for the weekend, waded across Duck Pond (Fletcher Lake) to buy the Asher Brown farm, consisting of 34 acres. Shortly after buying the farm, Bradner laid it out in building lots and called it Ocean Park. He built the Bradner Homestead in 1881 as a summer home. After his death, it was occupied by his widow, Mary H. Bradner, until her death on October 10, 1902. Bradner descendants still live in Bradley Beach and have been involved in all phases of the town's growth. (Courtesy Troy Bianchi.)

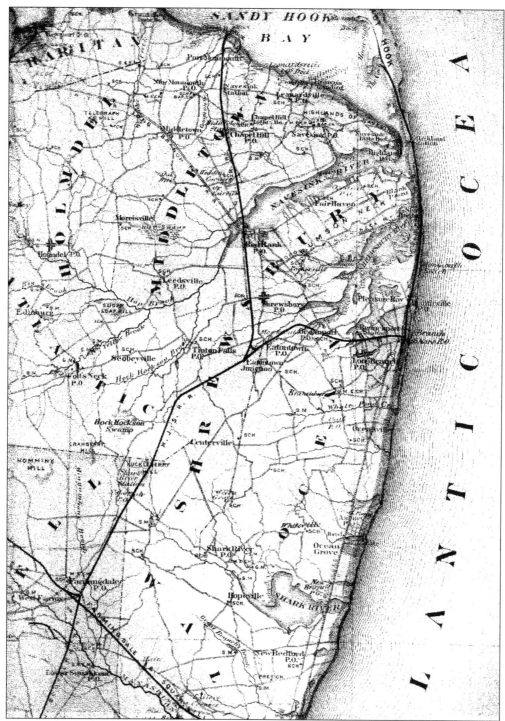

In the *F.W. Beers Atlas of Monmouth County, 1873*, Bradley Beach, or Ocean Park, was not even a name on the map. Fortunately, plans were being made and building lots drawn up by founders James A. Bradley and William B. Bradner. These two visionaries could see the potential that would be realized in a few short years. (Courtesy Ayres private collection.)

James A. Bradley, a wealthy brush manufacturer from lower Manhattan, in New York City, grew to love the idea of Ocean Grove as a religious retreat. Looking south across Duck Pond, Bradley saw potential in the land covered in sand dunes and pine forests. He purchased 500 acres in 1870 and, like Bradner, started laying out building lots and streets. Bradley gave away building lots to various religious organizations and to the library. For years, he patrolled the beaches, safeguarding bathers. Because of the vision of the two founders, Bradley Beach became a family resort before the beginning of the 20th century. (Courtesy Ayres private collection.)

Asbury Park resident Ella Mooney married William J. Paynter of Philadelphia at the Grand Avenue Reformed Church in July 1877 when she was 16 years old. James A. Bradley attended the wedding and took an interest in the young couple. Opening a clothing store on Main Street in Bradley's new development, Bradley Beach, the Paynters were soon out of business when their building burned. Bradley offered them a building lot at 900 Main Street and financial aid to build the new store. Elmer C. Bennett was the architect of the three-story Colonial-style structure, which had an elevator up to the third floor, where the Paynters had their apartment. Horse-drawn delivery carts enlarged their selling territory. The Paynters had the first motorcar, the first building lit by electricity, and the first telephone in town. William Paynter served as postmaster, town council member, bank vice president, board of education member, and almost everything else in town. Ella Paynter was instrumental in the development of the Methodist Church in Bradley Beach, as well as being a mother and serving as her husband's business partner. He lived to celebrate their 60th wedding anniversary and she lived another 10 years after that.

Two

Main Street, USA

Shown are borough hall and the fire department building in 1956, after the whole structure had been renovated, changing the equipment doors, removing the columns, and adding the municipal offices.

Bradley Beach, N. J., Nov 23rd 1895

Mr William B. Bradner Est

To The Mayor and Council of the Borough of Bradley Beach, Dr.

Valuation of Real Estate	Valuation of Personal Estate	Indebtedness	Levy	Poll Tax	State School	Special School Dist. 90½	Borough	County	Interest, Road Bonds & Poor	Amount of at $19.44 c $1,000
48.00						12.62	13.20	43.20	21.89	2.40	93.3

Tax, _____ 1893, _____ $ _____

Cost and Interest, = = = = = $ _____

Total, _____ $ _____

Received Payment. *William Larrabee* Collect.

This tax is now due and payable to Wm. Larrabee, Collector of Taxes of the Mayor and Council of the Borough of Bradley Beach, at office, Main Street, Bradley Beach, N. J., and **unless paid on or before the twentieth day of December, 1894,** will returned to a Justice of the Peace for prosecution, and on December 25, 1894, returned to the Collector with a Tax Warrant for collection. Twel per cent. interest and costs will be added to all taxes not paid by December 25, 1894. Taxes not paid by February 1, 1895, will be returned to County Clerk's office and filed as a first lien on real estate. The Commissioners of Appeal will be at Larrabee's Hall, Tuesday, November 27, 18 at 10 o'clock A.M.

Send 2-cent stamp for return postage.

WM. LARRABEE, Collector, Bradley Beach, N. J.

Penfield Pub. Co., Steam Printers, Asbury Park

The 1895 tax receipt for William B. Bradner's estate was for $93.31. William Larrabee was the tax collector, and a note at the bottom of the receipt claims that "The Commissioners of Appeal will be at Larrabee's Hall, Tuesday November 27, 1894 at 10 o'clock A.M. Send 2-cent stamp for return postage." Besides having no city hall at the time, the borough apparently had no budget for mail either. (Courtesy Florence K. Smith, Kirms family collection.)

Bradley Beach, N. J. *March 5th* 1897.

M *rs Elvira A. Bennett.*

To The Borough of Bradley Beach, Dr.

EDWARD YARNALL, Collector.

No. of Lots. 531	Valuation.	$	Cts.
and double house 1200.00			
Main St.			
Township Tax, ... $0.40 on $1,000			90
County Tax, ... 3.45 1,000		4	83
School, ... 6 70 1,000		4	03
State School, ... 2.45 1,000		3	39
Poll, ...			
Borough, ... 14.00 1,000		9	34
Amount of Tax		22	50
Cost and Interest		2	88
Tax, 1896 . . . *Cost of Sale*		25	38
Total Amount		2	73
		28	11

1895 tax

BRING OR SEND THIS BILL WITH YOUR PAYMENT.

Received payment, *Edward Yarnall* Collector.

$28.43

☞ **All Taxes must be paid on or before Dec. 20, 1897.** $28.43

Taxes not paid before December 20, 1897, will be returned to the Justice of the Peace, and on December 25, 1897. will be returned to the Collector in a Tax Warrant for collection. Six per cent interests and costs will be added to all taxes not paid by December 25, 1897.

Taxes not paid by February 1, 1898, will be returned to the County Clerk's office, and be filed as a first lien on real estate.

The Commissioners of Appeal will meet at the Council room on Main street, on Tuesday, November 23, 1897, at 9 A. M.

The Collector's office is at corner of Cook and Hammond avenues.

CHARLES WILKINS,
WILLIAM FURLONG, } Commissioners of Appeal. **EDWARD YARNALL, Collector,**

The March 1897 tax bill for Elvira A. Bennett's lot and double house at 531 Main Street was in the amount of $28.43. The property was assessed at $1,200. Edward Yarnall, tax collector, had his office on the corner of Cook (now LaReine) and Hammond Avenues. The borough offices were consolidated into one building when the new borough hall was built in 1908. (Courtesy Bradley Beach Historical Society collection.)

This picture of Main Street was taken *c.* 1910 looking north. In the foreground is Paynter's grocery store. The sidewalks are in place, even though the wide streets are unpaved. Huge utility poles stretch all the way north to Asbury Park, and lots of the houses and small businesses behind Paynter's store are making use of the new electric power flowing from the wires.

This 1970 view looking north on Main Street shows Schwarz Drug Store, formerly Paynter's grocery store, in the foreground. Borough workers are digging up the trolley car tracks. Although 900 Main Street still looks the same, most of the scenery has changed dramatically. Utility poles are on both sides of the street and handle a lot more than just electricity. Schwarz's has had a face-lift, with aluminum siding and new paint replacing the dark shingles and white paint that identified Paynter's store. Outwardly, the structure remains the same as when it was first built. (Courtesy Ayres private collection.)

This 1912 picture shows the First National Bank of Bradley Beach in its original setting, across from the railroad station on Main Street. In 1918, the bank moved into a new building on the corner of Brinley Avenue and Main Street. William Paynter was on the board of directors. On opening day, Raymond Johnson, a future teller of the bank, was first in line with his deposit. However, he stepped aside to allow Margaret Yarnell, Paynter's granddaughter, to be the first depositor. Neither Johnson nor Yarnell was tall enough to reach the window. (Courtesy Ayres private collection.)

Gloria Sciarappa stands in front of the family barbershop at 512 Main Street in 1944. The shop features a red-and-white striped barber pole, one of many visual aids used to advertise businesses in earlier times. (Courtesy William Sciarappa private collection.)

Wyckoff's Ice Cream Depot must have been a very popular place c. 1900, considering there was no air-conditioning at the time. It was located at 25 Main Street, in the southern part of town. During the summer, Wyckoff's used three horse-drawn carts to sell ice cream all over town, including the beachfront, which was starting to become a resort known to visitors from New Jersey and New York. (Courtesy Patty and Tom Rose.)

Members of Bradley Beach's dance orchestra, the Orioles, pose for a photograph c. 1928. The young men—Len Hauslet on drums, Mike Errico on guitar, John Cherry on piano, and Jerry Christian, John Giunco, and Pat Sciarappa on reeds and brass—played in Asbury Park nightclubs for many years. Giunco is the son of Vic Giunco, owner of Vic's Restaurant. The Sciarappa brothers built the addition to Vic's Restaurant in the 1960s. (Courtesy William Sciarappa private collection.)

This July 27, 1955 photograph was taken at the second annual Gay Nineties dance. From left to right are Lynda Baker, Miss Bradley Beach 1955; Commissioner Albert H. Kirms; Mrs. Sidney Ferman and her daughters Suzanne and Judy of Irvington; and Mayor Eugene Lowenstein, presenting the winning trophy to Mrs. Ferman. (Courtesy Florence K. Smith, Kirms family collection.)

This luncheonette and ice-cream parlor was at 510 Main Street, next to Fred Sciarappa's barbershop. Cesar Romero (later, an actor) was a steady customer. In this 1932 view, a very young William Sciarappa sits at the rear table. (Courtesy William Sciarappa private collection.)

The Bradley Palace movie theater ran an ad (left) in the December 20, 1925 issue of the *Asbury Park Press* for Rin-Tin-Tin, the "Marvel Dog," starring in *Below the Line*. Louise DeRose played the piano, and Mrs. DeRosa played the model 100-Special Wurlitzer pipe organ, newly installed for this movie. When sound movies came out in later years, the theater owners sold the organ, leaving only the air boxes (right) fastened to the walls. (Courtesy Ayres private collection.)

Built in the early 1920s, this theater featured vaudeville acts along with a silent movie and, until the organ was installed, the movies were accompanied by a piano. After renovations, it reopened as a movie theater on December 26, 1925. This view shows the Beach Cinema as it appears today. (Courtesy Ayres private collection.)

John Esposito, owner and operator of the Beach Cinema since December 1977, and his assistant Mary Mazza pose behind the candy counter. Two movie stars frequented this theater in their younger days: Jack Nicholson worked as an usher during his teenage years, and Cesar Romero watched many films here. (Courtesy Ayres private collection.)

During the depression years from the late 1920s to the mid 1930s, dinnerware was given away to movie patrons who presented their membership cards to be punched. What a bargain—the latest movie plus free dinnerware. At that time, the Palace Theater was part of the Arcadia Theatres chain of movies in the shore area. (Courtesy Bradley Beach Historical Society.)

Three

Vital Services

This is another view of the new borough center, with the fire equipment in front of the building. A close look reveals that the bell tower is empty and the weather vane has not been attached. Note the dentil molding around the windows and corners of the building. Next door is the Hotel LaReine, on the site that later became the addition to the hall and the parking lot. The hotel building was demolished after the LaReine reopened at an Ocean Avenue location *c.* 1900. (Courtesy Ayres private collection.)

A horse-drawn steam pumper, loaned to the Pioneer Fire Company in 1895 by the Ocean Grove Fire Department, takes part in the 1970 Memorial Day parade. When not in use, the equipment was stored in Councilman Peter Poland's barn. The first fire company of Bradley Beach was founded and organized on June 5, 1893. The first fire chief was Charles A. Bennett, who also served as the first constable of Bradley Beach. (Courtesy Bradley Beach Fire Department.)

THE
BOROUGH OF BRADLEY BEACH
OFFICE OF THE CLERK

H. C. PRATT, MAYOR
W. E. MACDONALD, CLERK
JOHN B. ROGERS, ASSESSOR
W. K. BRADNER, COLLECTOR
NIART ROGERS, CIVIL ENGINEER
AARON J. SMITH, RECORDER

Chairmen of Committees
JOS. T. STEWARD, FINANCE
E. B. FOSTER, STREET
WM. MATTHEWS, POLICE
GEO. H. BENNETT, FIRE & WATER
WM. MATTHEWS, ORDINANCE

BRADLEY BEACH, N. J.,

Oct. 20, 1902

Mr Joseph McDermott

Dear Sir

The following are the names of members of the Bradley Beach Fire Dept to which the Council granted exempt certificates

Henry P. Gant
Thomas P Barkalow
David F Gant
William W. Larrabee
Edward F Volhenus
William Brower
Timothy B Smith
J Edward Yarnall
Samuel Layton
Thomas Burney

Albert A Taylor
Charles Cooper
Joseph J Steward
Augustus J Jones
Alfred R Yarnall
William Gifford
William J Paynter
Peter O Rourke
Adam Harvey

Yours Truly
W E MacDonald
Borough Clerk

In this October 20, 1902 letter to Joseph McDermott of the fire department, W.E. MacDonald, borough clerk, grants exempt fireman certificates to 19 candidates. Exempt firemen were those who volunteered and served for a minimum of seven years and, thus, were no longer required to respond to fire calls—although most of them continued to do so. (Courtesy Bradley Beach Historical Society collection.)

Bradley Beach's unique Amoskeag fire engine is pictured in the official souvenir booklet of the state firemen's parade held on Friday, August 13, 1926, in Bradley Beach. Originally horse-drawn when purchased in 1908, the unit was rebuilt in 1921 with the forward portion of a Christie tractor into a one-of-a-kind self-propelled vehicle. The unit served for a total of 32 years before being retired in 1940. (Courtesy Bradley Beach Fire Department.)

Members of Pioneer Fire Company No. 1 appear in the souvenir booklet of the August 13, 1926 state firemen's parade. The doors of the building have been widened, and the ornamental molding above them has been filled in with bricks, leaving the shape of the missing piece still showing. (Courtesy Florence Kirms Smith, Kirms family collection.)

On the other side of the fire department's headquarters is the Independent Fire Company No. 2. Organized on February 10, 1897, the company purchased a new engine on March 1, 1897, for $1,350. Originally, each fire company was allowed 40 members, but when the short-lived Excelsior Fire Company merged with Independent, adding 25 members, the town council removed the membership restrictions. This picture is from the souvenir booklet of the August 13, 1926 state firemen's parade. (Courtesy Florence Kirms Smith, Kirms family collection.)

Bradley Fire Company No. 3 was added to the borough fire departments in 1908, when the eastern section of Neptune City voted to become part of Bradley Beach. The building was razed in 1999, after the borough decided to have only one fire company serve Bradley Beach. Currently proposed is a new fire headquarters for all the equipment and a much needed social section. This picture is from the souvenir booklet of the August 13, 1926 state firemen's parade. (Courtesy Florence Kirms Smith, Kirms family collection.)

THE BOARD OF COMMISSIONERS
OF THE
BOROUGH OF BRADLEY BEACH, N. J.

𝕿𝖍𝖎𝖘 𝖎𝖘 𝖙𝖔 𝖈𝖊𝖗𝖙𝖎𝖋𝖞 that   Albert Kirms   is an

EXEMPT FIREMAN

having served as a member of the Independent Fire Company in the Fire Department of the Borough of Bradley
Beach continuously for the term of seven years, is entitled to all the privileges and exemptions given him by law.

𝕴𝖓 𝖂𝖎𝖙𝖓𝖊𝖘𝖘 𝖂𝖍𝖊𝖗𝖊𝖔𝖋, the Borough of Bradley Beach has caused
these Presents to be signed by its Commissioners and attested by the Clerk, and
the corporate seal to be attached this ___Fifth___ day of June
One Thousand Nine Hundred and Thirty-four

_____ Clerk.   _____ Mayor.

_____ Commissioner.

_____ Commissioner.

Approved: _____ Chief.

This exempt fireman certificate was issued to Albert Kirms, who served seven years with
Independent Fire Company No. 2. Dated June 5, 1934, the certificate is signed by Frank C.
Borden, the mayor from 1919 to 1943, and by Commissioner Bernard V. Poland, a relative of
Councilman Peter Poland, who housed fire equipment in his barn in 1895. (Courtesy Florence
Kirms Smith, Kirms family collection.)

The bell was taken from the tower of the razed fire department and placed in the park to honor the heroes from all three fire departments. (Courtesy Bradley Beach Historical Society collection.)

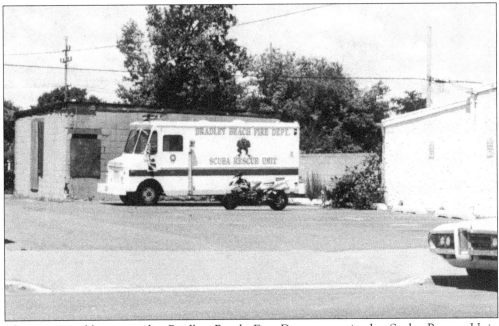

The newest addition to the Bradley Beach Fire Department is the Scuba Rescue Unit, established in 1990. (Courtesy Ayres private collection.)

This 1956 photograph shows Mayor Albert H. Kirms (right) presenting Fire Chief Charles M. "Bud" Cozzens with the keys to the new fire truck. (Courtesy Florence Kirms Smith, Kirms family collection.)

Members of the fire department pose in 1956 with their newest piece of equipment. (Courtesy Florence Kirms Smith, Kirms family collection.)

Commissioner Albert H. Kirms (left) presents members of Pioneer Fire Company No. 1 with the keys to the new GMC Seagrave aerial truck in May 1965. (Courtesy Florence Kirms Smith, Kirms family collection.)

Walter Wilson, Bradley Beach fire chief, poses with the chief's command vehicle in 2000. (Courtesy Walter Wilson collection.)

Fire Chief Walter Wilson is pictured in 2000. (Courtesy Walter Wilson collection.)

John Zech, Bradley Beach fire chief in 2002, gives Leo the fire dog a seat on the Seagrave fire engine owned by Hamilton, in Neptune Township. Leo holds full membership in the Bradley Beach Fire Department and even has a badge.

The newest equipment of Bradley Beach Fire Department No. 2 takes part in the 1970 Memorial Day parade on Main Street.

For the 1970 Memorial Day parade, Engine Company No. 1 proudly displays an American flag on its newest piece of equipment.

On April 19, 1893, the council authorized the office of marshal, thereby establishing what eventually became the Bradley Beach Police Department. The first marshal was Charles A. Bennett, earning badge No. 1. His assigned schedule was to work six months of day shifts and six months of night shifts. In later years he was appointed the first constable, the first policeman, and the first fire chief.

The police department in 1928 still included Charles Bennett, shown in the middle of the first row. (Courtesy John B. Gregg.)

Police officers Poland, Neuhouse, Conveny, and Caporn stand with the police department's new patrol cars in 1936.

On Memorial Day of 1934, six Bradley Beach officials pose in front of the municipal office doors. They are identified only as Rogers, Poland, Mayor Frank C. Borden, Farry, Bernie Poland, and Reichey.

In 1915, two of the police department's new recruits were Harry Francis and Charles Poland.

This photograph, taken on Memorial Day in 1930, shows a large contingent of the police department. Some of the officers are special policemen hired for summertime beach-patrol duty.

Members of the police department pose for a Memorial Day photograph on May 31, 1954. Behind them is the entrance to the police department. Also on this side of the borough complex is a door (left) leading to the stairway up to the second-floor municipal offices. (Courtesy Florence Kirms Smith, Kirms family collection.)

On duty in 1956, Sgt. Charles M. "Bud" Cozzens patrols on a motorcycle. Originally, police officers patrolled the borough on foot or by bicycle. Today, bicycle and motorized cycle teams patrol the boardwalk and Ocean Avenue during the summer. Cozzens, a lifelong resident of Bradley Beach, was a veteran of World War II and a member of the Bradley Beach First Aid and Fire Departments. He joined the police department in 1947. While on duty on August 8, 1964, he died in a single-car accident involving his police car. (Courtesy Florence Kirms Smith, Kirms family collection.)

The police department poses for a group picture in 1959. Following an addition to the building in 1956, the municipal offices moved to the other side of the building. In this picture, therefore, the only door on the side of the building is for the police department. (Courtesy Florence Kirms Smith, Kirms family collection.)

In a ceremony on February 23, 1965, Commissioner Albert H. Kirms (left) promotes Sgt. John B. Gregg to lieutenant as Police Chief Harvey Gaunt looks on. (Courtesy Florence Kirms Smith, Kirms family collection.)

Harvey T. Gaunt poses on December 31, 1971, the date of his retirement from the police force. Gaunt, the third duly appointed police chief, served 20 years beginning in 1951. He is pictured in front of a plaque honoring Mayor Eugene Lowenstein.

At his retirement dinner, Harvey T. Gaunt was presented with a special cake in the shape of a police chief's cap.

Councilman Albert H. Kirms is pictured in a 1965 portrait. (Courtesy Florence Kirms Smith, Kirms family collection.)

Dressed in their summer uniforms, members of the police department pose in Railroad Park in front of the obelisk on Memorial Day in 1968. Notice their white gloves.

Members of the police department display their riot gear in this photograph taken on March 28, 1971. During a period of racial unrest, Bradley Beach police officers were called to help patrol Springwood Avenue in Asbury Park. Most of the buildings on that avenue were burned to the ground or razed, leaving nothing standing. Some 30 years later, this once bustling business section is still deserted and in ruins. (Courtesy John B. Gregg.)

Commissioner Albert H. Kirms (left) and Police Chief Harvey Gaunt stand by an ambulance that has been converted into a police riot vehicle.

As part of crime-fighting awareness week, the police visit the Bradley Beach Grammar School. Officer Siciliano, as McGruff the crime-fighter, is flanked by officers Scully, Leather, and Fromholz in this April 12, 1988 photograph. (Courtesy Bradley Beach Historical Society collection.)

The Bradley Beach First Aid Squad was organized in May 1933 under the auspices of the Ladies Auxiliary of the Bradley Beach Fire Department. Watson MacInnes was named the first president. A requirement for membership was membership in the fire department. The 1929 Studebaker hearse was purchased from Farry Funeral Home with the help of the auxiliary. The vehicle was refurbished and used to transport the sick and injured to Fitkin Hospital in Neptune. (Courtesy Bradley Beach First Aid Squad.)

Lots 725 through 727 on Main Street were purchased from the Webb Building and Loan Association on April 5, 1939. Construction of the Bradley Beach First Aid Squad building began on October 19, 1941, and was completed and dedicated on February 4, 1942. In 1948, the squad reorganized and incorporated itself, independent of the fire department. In its nearly 70 years of operation, the squad has answered calls for major disasters, including the Hindenburg dirigible explosion at Lakehurst in 1937. (Courtesy Ayres private collection.)

Deutsche Zeppelin-Reederei
GMBH

Direktion

An

First Aid & Ambulance Corps,
Bradley Beach Department, Inc.,

Bradley Beach, New Jersey
U.S.A.

Sehr geehrte Herren !

Bei der Durchsicht des umfangreichen, uns zur Verfügung gestellten
Materials an Berichten über den Unfall von Lakehurst entnehmen wir
zu unserer grossen Freude, dass sich das

First Aid & Ambulance Corps, Bradley Beach

durch die einsatzbereite Hilfe und die kameradschaftliche Unter-
stützung bei dem tragischen Unglück von Lakehurst am 6. Mai 1937
ausgezeichnet hat.

Es ist uns ein Bedürfnis, Ihnen unseren verbindlichen Dank auszu-
sprechen für alles, was Sie und Ihre Helfer bei der Bergung der
Verunglückten geleistet haben und dafür, dass Sie durch Ihren so-
fortigen Beistand zur Linderung der Schmerzen beigetragen haben.
Sie haben durch diesen Beweis Ihrer Pflichterfüllung und aufopfern-
den Nächstenliebe einen grossen Dienst nicht nur den Verletzten
selbst, sondern auch damit unserer Gesellschaft und weiten Kreisen
der Luftfahrt erwiesen, für den wir Ihnen von Herzen dankbar sind.

Wir bitten Sie, den Dank unserer Gesellschaft auch den einzelnen
Helfern Ihrer Organisation zu übermitteln.

Mit vorzüglicher Hochachtung !
Deutsche Zeppelin-Reederei
G.m.b.H.

In appreciation of the help from the Bradley Beach First Aid Squad during the Hindenburg disaster, the Zeppelin Company in Germany sent this letter on September 14, 1937. (Courtesy Bradley Beach Historical Society.)

Bradley Beach First Aid Squad, Inc.

Bradley Beach, New Jersey

Translated from a letter from Frankfurt, Germany
on A.M., 14 September 1937

Dear Sirs:

Checking the voluminous reports covering the
accident at Lakehurst, we are very happy to see
that the First Aid and Ambulance Corps, Bradley
Beach was outstanding through their energetic and
courageous help at the tragic accident at Lakehurst
on May 6, 1937.

We wish to thank you and your assistants for
rendering First Aid to the people involved in this
accident and for your invaluable assistance in
recovering these wounded people. Through your help
you have done an important service, not only for
the victims, but also for our Company and for many
people in our Aircraft industry. We thank you very
much.

Please give the thanks of our Company also to
all the assistants of your organization.

Very truly,

Your German-Zeppelin Company

This is a direct translation of the Zeppelin Company letter that appears on page 53. (Courtesy Bradley Beach Historical Society.)

Members of the Bradley Beach First Aid Squad pose in 1956 with their two ambulances. They wear the uniform of the day: white shirt, khaki pants, and a white baseball cap with a red cross on it. (Courtesy Florence Kirms Smith, Kirms family collection.)

In 1880, the New York and Long Branch Railroad extended its service south to Bradley Beach, and the newly discovered resort town came to life. Summer visitors flocked to the beaches on crowded trains. Previously, the only transportation from New York and northern New Jersey had been by horse-drawn coach, which took up to two days over mud-choked and rutted roads. The train ride took only a few hours and it brought not just visitors but also profitable freight. Before major highways were built and then used by trucks, trains brought building materials, food, and the mail. City dwellers began to buy houses at the shore, preferring to commute to work by train. Bradley Beach founder James Bradley fought hard against having trains stop at the railroad depot on Sunday. His argument was that once the trains stopped in town, "the next thing you know they'll be bathing on Sunday afternoon." (Courtesy Bradley Beach Historical Society.)

The southbound *Blue Comet Nostalgia Special* approaches the Fourth Avenue crossing in December 1975. (Courtesy Gary S. Crawford private collection.)

The Bradley Beach freight station was actually on the west side of the yard, in Neptune. The building is pictured in November 1972, just before it was demolished. Memorial Drive runs through this location today. (Courtesy Gary S. Crawford private collection.)

This view, looking from across the park to the train station, shows commuters waiting for the city-bound train. (Courtesy Ayres private collection.)

This building was once a two-stall trolley carbarn, with repair shop and garage for trolley cars. Today, it is National Cash & Carry, a retail distributor of food and paper products. (Courtesy Ayres private collection.)

Four

THE LIBRARY, THE ELEMENTARY SCHOOL, AND THE POST OFFICE

In 1913, the Women's Improvement League held a house-to-house canvas for new and used books to start a library collection. During its first year, the public library operated out of a room in the grammar school. James A. Bradley donated land at the southeast corner of Fourth and Hammond Avenues to be used expressly for the construction of a library building. Architect E.H. Schmieder and builder H.H. Moore Inc. constructed the Colonial building with an Indiana limestone front and a marble entrance, featuring double 12-foot-tall brass-and-metal alloy plating over wooden-core doors. The total cost was $50,000. The library was dedicated on December 1, 1927. Two large bronze tablets hang in the foyer, facing each other. One is a memorial to the 165 men from Bradley Beach who served in World War I, and the other contains the names of the library officers, commissioners, architect, and builder. (Courtesy Ayres private collection.)

In 1972, the library was reconditioned and modernized, and the children's section was moved to a large room in the basement. The details on the columns and pediment can be seen. Not seen in this picture are the brass doors, which were restored to their original luster in 2001. (Courtesy Ayres private collection.)

The library staff and director Bert LePree celebrate the 60th anniversary of the library by throwing a party for the town. The mayor, the town council members, the library board, and many residents showed up for this happy event in 1987. (Courtesy Ayres private collection.)

SOUVENIR CIRCUS COLORING BOOK

COMPLIMENTS OF

BRADLEY BEACH PUBLIC LIBRARY

AND

CIRCUS FANS OF AMERICA.

FIRST ANNUAL CIRCUS WEEK

AUGUST 17 to 22, 1987.

As part of the 60th anniversary of the library in 1987, a souvenir circus coloring book was given out to visitors. The Circus Fans of America club brought displays and exhibits to the library and talked about circus life. (Courtesy Bradley Beach Historical Society collection.)

TAKE A KID TO A CIRCUS!

This is a detail from the souvenir coloring book. Circus Fans of America members Tom Salisbury and Todd Robinson were on hand all week to answer questions and describe the daily life of circus employees. (Courtesy Bradley Beach Historical Society collection.)

The first public school classes were held above a Main Street store. Two sets of students were taught by one teacher. In 1883, a small wooden structure was built on the east side of Main Street between Evergreen and Monmouth Avenues—a portion of Bradley Beach that was part of Neptune City until 1908. A newer school was built in 1886 on Fifth Avenue. This small wooden structure, with three rooms upstairs and three rooms downstairs, served greater Bradley Beach. Classes up to the fourth-grade level were held, and students then paid tuition to transfer to either Asbury Park or Neptune schools. In 1904, the school board took over the school, refusing to send any more elementary students to other districts. The board severed connections with the Neptune school district and decided to run its own district. (Courtesy Ayres private collection.)

As the need for a larger and safer building arose, a new school was built in 1911 on Brinley Avenue. Building costs, including landscaping and sidewalks, came to $87,000. The school was constructed of buff bricks with brownstone corners and a variegated slate roof. The floors were reinforced concrete, and all doors and partitions and girders were of fireproof materials. On the second floor was an auditorium with a seating capacity of 750. In 1911, the president of the board of education was Dr. Wesley K. Bradner, son of Bradley Beach founder William Bradner. On the school building committee was William J. Paynter. In 1927, a large gymnasium was built and over it, in 1960, a new wing of the school was added. (Courtesy Ayres private collection.)

When movie actor Cesar Romero was a boy, he and his family moved from Manhattan to this home in Bradley Beach. Romero graduated from Bradley Beach Elementary School in June 1922 and, after he graduated from high school, the family moved to California so that he could pursue an acting career. The rest, as they say, is history. (Courtesy Bradley Beach Historical Society collection.)

The Bradley Beach Alumni and Grammar School Band played not only for school functions but also in borough parades. The band is pictured in 1938, with Principal Grandi in the back row, second from the left. (Courtesy William Sciarappa.)

Memorial Day services featuring the Bradley Beach Grammar School band take place in Railroad Park. The date was May 30, 1959. (Courtesy Florence Kirms Smith, Kirms family collection.)

The Tri-Boro Little League (Bradley Beach, Avon, and Neptune City) opens its season at the recreation center. Seen across Main Street in this June 1964 view is Saltzman's store. Members of the winning team obtained their victory sodas at Saltzman's. (Courtesy Florence Kirms Smith, Kirms family collection.)

The first post office was established in a store on Newark Avenue, with Catherine E. Bickerton as the first postmaster. In 1894, the post office moved to Paynter's grocery store on Main Street, with William Paynter as the postmaster. State Sen. Oscar Brown installed 13-year-old Margretta Paynter as assistant postmaster. At that time, mail was dropped off at the Bradley Beach railroad station instead of Asbury Park. City mail delivery was started in 1918. (Courtesy Ayres private collection.)

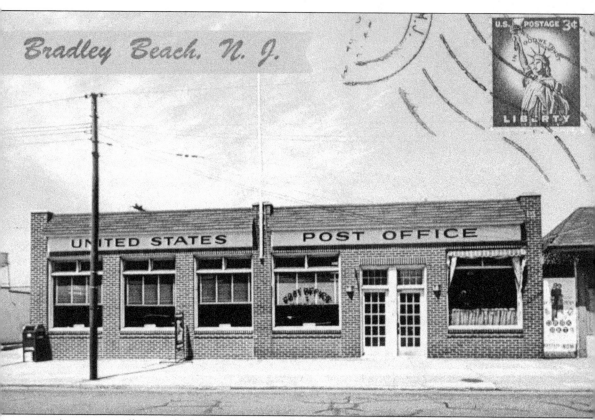

A new post office was built in 1938 at 517 Main Street, its present location. A large addition was completed in 1953, and general improvements were made during 2000. (Courtesy Ayres private collection.)

The Freedom Train came to Bradley Beach on Labor Day weekend of 1976, during the nation's bicentennial. The steam locomotive was a former Reading Railroad engine built in 1945 and refitted for the special 18,000-mile journey around the country. It had 10 exhibit cars and 2 showcase cars. Each of the 10 cars was equipped with a moving walkway from which the exhibits were viewed. (Courtesy Milton Edelman collection.)

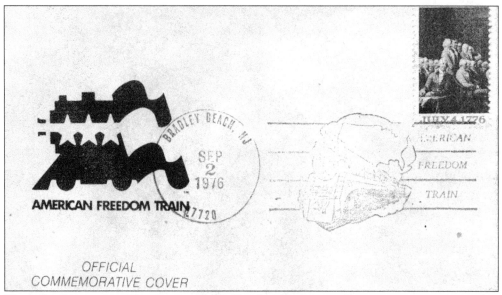

OFFICIAL
COMMEMORATIVE COVER

This official commemorative cover with the Freedom Train cancellation was sent on September 2, 1976, from the Bradley Beach substation at the Freedom Train location. The substation, a postal truck with an awning over the open back door, was staffed by Bradley Beach Postmaster Lyman Graham and clerks Kim Trimble and Robert Smith. All sales bore a Bradley Beach postmark with a replica of the train. (Courtesy Ayres private collection.)

The American Freedom Train, 26 red-white-and-blue cars pulled by a 425-ton Reading steam engine, arrived in Bradley Beach at 9:30 a.m. Thursday, September 2, 1976. The public viewed exhibits on a moving walkway in the 10 display cars. Car No. 1, the Beginning, showed America's achievements, spanning two centuries. Car No. 2, Exploration and Expansion, highlighted America's expansion from the days of westward movement to the space program. Car No. 3, Growth of a Nation, displayed the transformation of America's landscape from wilderness to skyscrapers. Car No. 4, Origins, represented the broad cultural mix of America. Car No. 5, Innovations, exhibited inventions and machinery. Car No. 6, Human Resources, represented the country's diversity of trades. Car No. 7, Sports, re-created some of the great moments in American sports. Car No. 8, Performing Arts, highlighted the history of Hollywood. Car No. 9, Fine Arts, displayed works of the nation's artists, sculptors, and composers. Car 10, Conflict and Resolution, portrayed various times of crisis in American history. (Courtesy Milton Edelman private collection.)

Three Neptune Township officials stand behind the commemorative plaque placed at the railroad siding where the Freedom Train was parked for the weekend. From left to right are Al Bennett, clerk; Almerth Battle, township committee; and A.L. Ward, police chief. Officials from Neptune, Bradley Beach, and Asbury Park were on hand for opening ceremonies. (Courtesy Ayres private collection.)

The American Freedom Train

Monmouth-Ocean Freedom Train Committee, Inc.

c/o Monmouth-Ocean Development Council
601 Bangs Avenue (Suite 905-906)
Asbury Park, New Jersey 07712
(201) 776-6666

United States 13c

Post Master Lyman H. Graham

Bradley Beach Post Office

Bradley Beach, N. J. 07720

This envelope was sent to Postmaster Lyman Graham from the Monmouth-Ocean Freedom Train Committee on September 24, 1976. (Courtesy Ayres private collection.)

Five

CHINATOWN-BY-THE-SEA

In 1922, the Church of All Nations in lower Manhattan opened Cliff Villa, a summer getaway at 110 Cliff Avenue in Bradley Beach. The house was for residents of Chinatown, Little Italy, and other ethnic neighborhoods, with the first three weeks of summer for the Chinese, the second three weeks for the Italians, and the final three weeks for other groups. In a personal note to Shirley Ayres, Bruce Edward Hall, author of *Tea That Burns* (Free Press, 1998), wrote: "[As it does for] other descendents of the early settlers of New York's Chinatown, Bradley Beach holds a special place in my family's memory. In the decades after the First World War, the social life of Mott Street was transferred lock, stock, and barrel to sleepy Newark Avenue in this tiny hamlet on the shore. My great aunts and their friends would blissfully surrender themselves to marathon games of mah jongg, while the men would pile into my grandfather's LaSalle and head off to bet on the horses at Monmouth Park. Once in a while they even went to the beach. The younger generation would partake of the wonders that Asbury Park and the ocean had to offer, timidly staying out of sight when the white kids would have dances in the Pavilion. 'It's not that we weren't invited', one cousin remembers. 'It's that we were afraid of being made fun of.' Meanwhile, second-generation Italians spent their summers a block away on Ocean Park Place in a surreal [re-creation] of lower Manhattan. Just as in New York City, the two groups lived side by side, each more or less ignoring the other." (Courtesy Ayres private collection.)

The Church of All Nations in lower Manhattan, a Methodist church, served the needs of the immigrants in the area. Behind the double red doors were a huge pool, a gym area, day-care facilities, a kitchen, and the church.

Cliff Villa was run by director Thelma Burdick and her assistant, Joe Giglia. Giglia and his wife, Bea (pictured), stayed in Bradley Beach all summer, overseeing the daily operations, which included scheduling the ringing of the bell for meals by the resident children. (Courtesy Ayres private collection.)

Bea Giglia leans out the second-floor screen door to call the guests in for lunch. The door was all that was left of a small porch, removed when the roof was replaced. (Courtesy Ayres private collection.)

The house on Cliff Avenue overlooked Fletcher Lake and was two short blocks from the ocean. The station wagon, used by assistant Joe Giglia to get supplies and pick up visitors at the train station, displays a sign for Cliff Villa. In 1964, after a lengthy illness, director Thelma Burdick sold Cliff Villa to Joe and Bea Giglia, who were living full time in Bradley Beach. Unfortunately, an arsonist burned the house to the ground in the winter of 1965, leaving nothing but memories of the four decades during which Cliff Villa had been host to so many city visitors. The Giglia's daughter Gloria Weilandis and her family still live on Newark Avenue. (Courtesy Ayres private collection.)

In the early 1940s, Lee B. Lok and his wife, Ng Shee, became the first Chinese family to buy a house in Bradley Beach. The family, introduced to the area by a stay at Cliff Villa, had rented rooms on Newark Avenue. One day Lee Ng Shee was walking along the street when a woman came out on her porch and asked, "Are you looking for a house? Would you like to buy this one?" and $2,000 later, the Lee family owned a home in Bradley Beach. After that, more and more Chinese families bought homes on Newark Avenue, thus creating the community that became known as Chinatown-by-the-Sea. The Lee house, at 104 Newark Avenue, is still owned by granddaughter Pat Lee, an art teacher in Neptune Township. (Courtesy Pat Lee family collection.)

This closeup of the Lee family house on Newark Avenue shows how it looks today. (Courtesy Bradley Beach Historical Society collection.)

Six

BRADLEY BEACH
GETS RELIGION

When James A. Bradley and William Bradner founded Bradley Beach in the 1870s, the area had only a few farms. The rest was sand dunes and pine woods, where small animals lived. To the north and just over Duck Pond, now known as Fletcher Lake, lay the newly created religious settlement of Ocean Grove, with St. Paul's Methodist Church as its center. Bradley and Bradner, visitors to Ocean Grove, thought of their newly acquired property as part of the Camp Meeting's territory. When the need arose in Bradley Beach for a church of its own, Bradley not only donated the property but also arranged to have the Old Dutch Reformed Church moved here from Asbury Park. The Little Church in the Woods, as worshippers called it, was dedicated in June 1886. The new First Methodist Church was dedicated in November 1900, with Ella and William Paynter instrumental in the organization. The church recently celebrated its centennial. (Courtesy Bradley Beach Historical Society collection.)

The second church in Bradley Beach was the Roman Catholic Church of the Ascension, on Brinley Avenue. Previous to its erection, parishioners had to walk to the Catholic church in North Asbury. In 1907, the Bradley Beach parish was formed, celebrating masses at the LaReine Casino on Ocean Avenue. Plans were drawn up by Philadelphia architect George I. Lovatt for the new church. The cornerstone was laid on July 3, 1910, and the church was dedicated on June 25, 1911. Movie stars Jack Nicholson and Cesar Romero were members of this church. (Courtesy Ayres private collection.)

Mayor Albert H. Kirms (center) breaks ground for the new recreation center of Ascension Church c. 1957. (Courtesy Florence Kirms Smith, Kirms family collection.)

Sponsored by the Trinity Church in Asbury Park, St. James Episcopal Church began as a trial mission, moving from storefront to homes and back to Main Street before James Bradley contributed ground at Fourth and Hammond Avenues. On October 14, 1916, the cornerstone was laid for the new church and, in January 1917, the building was dedicated. St. James continued as a mission church until May 1946, when it became a parish church. (Courtesy Ayres private collection.)

In the 1920s, a Jewish study group held meetings in a privately owned rooming house at 200 McCabe Avenue. When the rooming house was sold, the group purchased a lot on the corner of McCabe and Central Avenues to erect a synagogue. In 1926, the members organized and established the Congregation Agudath Achim of Bradley Beach. Many of its members worked at nearby Fort Monmouth as engineers and communication specialists. (Courtesy Ayres private collection.)

In 1960, the cornerstone was laid for the Florence Warner Community Center and, in 1962, the building was completed. The congregation consists mostly of first- and second-generation Russian and Eastern European immigrants. The synagogue owns a cemetery on West Bangs Avenue in Neptune, which has been in use since the early 1950s. Summer visitor Ed Koch, the former mayor of New York, attended the synagogue. (Courtesy Ayres private collection.)

In the early 1930s, a few families from the Magen David community of Brooklyn came to spend summers in Bradley Beach. Being orthodox Sephardic Jews, they decided a house of worship was needed. They formed the Magen David Congregation of Bradley Beach, secured property on the corner of Fifth and Ocean Avenues, and built a synagogue and study halls in the 1940s. In the 1960s, they undertook an expansion and modernization program designed to benefit all members, with a strong emphasis on the youth of the congregation. In the late 1970s, a large group from the congregation moved a few miles north to Deal and remained there. The year-round members attend services at the Congregation Agudath Achim during the winter and open their building during the summer. (Courtesy Ayres private collection.)

The congregation of Kingdom Hall of Jehovah's Witnesses began holding services in a Belmar storefront near Freedman's bakery. In 1953, the members of the Homer family of Neptune City donated land on Main Street in Bradley Beach as the site for a house of worship. The Regional Building Committee for the Jehovah's Witnesses in the state of New Jersey planned and organized all details for the new building. The only expense was for materials, as labor was furnished by members skilled in the building trades. The work was done on weekends, and the building went up in a matter of months. The regional committee came back to Bradley Beach when the need arose for renovations. The work, including landscaping, was completed in three months, and the renovated site was dedicated on November 18, 2001. (Courtesy Ayres private collection.)

THE BRADLEY BEACH

KINGDOM HALL

OF JEHOVAH'S WITNESSES

INVITE YOU TO A

DEDICATION CEREMONY

SUNDAY, NOVEMBER 18, 2001

TO BEGIN AT

9:00 AM

28 MAIN STREET

BRADLEY BEACH, NJ

DEDICATION PROGRAM ON REVERSE

This is an invitation to the dedication ceremony of the renovated Kingdom Hall of Jehovah's Witnesses on Sunday, November 18, 2001. (Courtesy Ayres private collection.)

Seven

OCEAN AVENUE

The luxurious LaReine Hotel, built in 1900, was a summer home to many visitors. Cesar Romero, a guest one summer after he became a movie star, talked to lifeguard Jack Nicholson about a common interest: acting. The hotel was destroyed by fire in 1974. (Courtesy Ayres private collection.)

LaReine Hotel employee Richard Klein, a professional trainer, leads a group in calisthenics on the beach c. 1927. Bradley Beach was the first community in the country to charge admission to restricted beaches. The plan to sell beach tags was developed here in 1928 or 1929 and, afterward, was adopted elsewhere in the country. This picture was taken before the wearing of badges became part of the beach scene. (Courtesy Bradley Beach Historical Society collection.)

This early morning fire in April 1974 destroyed not only the beautiful LaReine Hotel but also the adjoining Bradley Hotel. (Courtesy Todd Robinson collection.)

The Gun Club held its meetings in this Ocean Avenue house, pictured c. 1930. Originally a private home, the building was taken over by the American Legion at the beginning of World War II, after the Gun Club moved its meetings to borough hall. The house was destroyed by a storm in the late 1950s. (Courtesy William Sciarappa private collection.)

The first house in Bradley Beach was that of the Kent family. Built in the 1880s, the ornate structure had the Atlantic Ocean across the street and Fletcher Lake in its backyard. Notice the lack of houses on the lake. (Courtesy Ayres private collection.)

In the 1890s, the Kent house was sold and converted to the Lakensea Hotel. Guest rooms were added to the structure, as seen in this view, and it became a very popular place to stay. The hotel burned to the ground in the 1950s, and garden apartments were built on the property. (Courtesy Ayres private collection.)

Today, garden apartments stand on the site of the former Kent house and Lakensea Hotel. (Courtesy Bradley Beach Historical Society collection.)

Built at the north end of Bradley Beach in the early part of the 20th century, the Beach View Hotel was situated right on the beach. Guests could step off the wraparound porch onto the sand. (Courtesy Ayres private collection.)

The Beach View Hotel had its own swimming pool. In later years, the hotel was destroyed by a storm. Today, a parking lot has taken its place. (Courtesy Ayres private collection.)

In this 1920s beach scene, the LaReine Hotel looms in the background and the memorial statue to the *New Era*, a ship destroyed by a storm off Bradley Beach in 1854, stands on the sand. (Courtesy Ayres private collection.)

The wooden *New Era* seaman, on the beach between Newark and Ocean Park Avenues, is dedicated to the passengers and crew and Captain White's rescue team from Long Branch. The statue shows a seaman on top of an actual mast from the wrecked ship. Sometimes called the "Old Salt," the statue was dismantled in the 1930s. (Courtesy Ayres private collection.)

This *c.* 1910 Ocean Avenue view, looking south from Brinley Avenue, shows a light fixture in the middle of the street. Fixtures such as this one caused many automobile accidents before they were removed. (Courtesy Ayres private collection.)

This 1994 photograph shows the Ocean Avenue light fixture restructured to become part of the dolphin fountain located across from the former Grossman and LaReine Hotels, now condominiums. (Courtesy Ayres private collection.)

By September 2000, the fountain fixture has been restructured and now bears no resemblance to the base of the Ocean Avenue light stanchion. (Courtesy Ayres private collection.)

This fountain in the courtyard dining room of Vic's Restaurant looks a lot like the dolphin fountain on Ocean Avenue.

This 1994 photograph shows the dolphin statue being repositioned. Its fountain had been weakened by the 1992 northeast storm that destroyed most of the boardwalk, the pool, and the Fourth Avenue pavilion on the east side of Ocean Avenue. (Courtesy Bradley Beach Historical Society collection.)

A new gazebo was built in 1993 for the east side of Ocean Avenue at Fifth Avenue, the former site of the tennis courts that were destroyed by a storm in the 1940s. (Courtesy Bradley Beach Historical Society collection.)

Borough workers were the construction crew for the Ocean Avenue gazebo built in July 1993, as well as for other projects throughout the town. (Courtesy Bradley Beach Historical Society collection.)

This 1993 photograph shows the Fifth Avenue gazebo nearly completed. The entire boardwalk had to be repositioned and rebuilt due to the extensive storm damage. (Courtesy Bradley Beach Historical Society collection.)

On summer evenings under the decorative three-tiered roof of the gazebo, musicians gather to play live music of all types for listening and dancing. The gazebo has also been the site of marriage ceremonies. Mostly, however, it is a prime place for borough residents and visitors to sit and enjoy the ocean view. (Courtesy Ayres private collection.)

Four days after the September 11, 2001 terrorist attack, borough officials and private citizens held a memorial to all those who suffered and died that tragic day. The gazebo was decorated with flags and flowers donated by Lori Torres, owner of the Bradley Garden Florist Shop. (Courtesy Ayres private collection.)

The hurricane of September 1944 left heavy damage in its wake. This view shows the north end of Ocean Avenue and what was once the boardwalk. The roof of the gazebo lies in the middle of the road. Across Fletcher Lake is Ocean Grove. Hurricanes were not named until 1950 and then, for many years, only the names of women were used. (Courtesy Bradley Beach Historical Society collection.)

In November 1935, a northeastern storm roared up the New Jersey coast, causing millions of dollars in damage. The storm rolled 10-ton rocks out of the Manasquan Inlet into the ocean. Bradley Beach lost most of its beach sand, as the shore was stripped down to marl. The Jersey Central trains were unable to run due to storm-twisted tracks. Although the pavilions and the LaReine Hotel (background) look untouched by the storm, almost every structure along the beachfront was damaged. (Courtesy Bradley Beach Historical Society collection.)

This February 27, 1954 photograph shows damage to the boardwalk, exposing support joists. (Courtesy Florence Kirms Smith, Kirms family collection.)

This view shows damage to the Fourth Avenue Pavilion from a 1944 northeast storm. (Courtesy Bradley Beach Historical Society collection.)

After a December 1992 storm, all that remains of the boardwalk at Fourth and Fifth Avenues are sticks. (Courtesy Bradley Beach Public Library collection.)

A 1944 storm has strewn parts of the boardwalk across Ocean Avenue and a lawn. This view was taken looking north toward the Fourth Avenue pavilion. (Courtesy Bradley Beach Historical Society collection.)

Taken from the jetty, this February 1955 view shows an extremely low tide and the American Legion building. A few sea gulls are the only sign of life on the beachfront. The area was still recovering from Hurricane Edna, which struck in September 1954. (Courtesy Bradley Beach Historical Society collection.)

Some of Hurricane Edna's damage is seen in this February 1955 photograph. A large portion of the southern end of the boardwalk has been ripped off, and gouges in the sand are still visible. (Courtesy Bradley Beach Historical Society collection.)

Before the terrible damage done to the boardwalk and oceanfront by the December 1992 storm, an adult physical fitness course was held at the Third Avenue boardwalk. (Courtesy Bradley Beach Historical Society collection.)

This bocce court was added to the oceanfront area in the 1980s. Another set of courts, with a small gazebo, was added in 2002. Bocce leagues run during the summer months, and the sport is popular year-round. (Courtesy Bradley Beach Historical Society collection.)

One of the big events in Bradley Beach was the bicycle race. This July 4, 1913 photograph shows Naph Poland, manager of the road race, with the field of racers. It was taken on the McCabe Avenue side of the Bradley Inn, which still stands today. Poland owned a bicycle shop at 812 Main Street. (Courtesy Bradley Beach Historical Society collection.)

Except for the siding and the roof, the Bradley Inn of today appears the same as it did some 90 years ago. (Courtesy Bradley Beach Historical Society collection.)

The LaReine Casino housed five concessions and a dance hall. Shown *c.* 1910, the building was destroyed by fire in April 1932. (Courtesy Bradley Beach Historical Society collection.)

In this *c.* 1910 view, the LaReine Casino is in the background, the merry-go-round in the left foreground, and the bowling alley across from the casino in the background. The structures extended east across Ocean Avenue. (Courtesy Bradley Beach Historical Society collection.)

This view offers a closer look at the bowling alley in Bradley Beach. (Courtesy Bradley Beach Historical Society collection.)

This *c.* 1900 scene shows the bathhouse next to the brick "boardwalk," with steps down to the sand. On the beach are boats and private wagons, along with the poles and ropes for the safety of bathers. (Courtesy Bradley Beach Historical Society collection.)

This 1910 photograph shows equipment of Fire Company No. 3: a horse-drawn gasoline-powered unit with the pump engine over the rear wheels. This was the first gasoline-powered unit purchased for Bradley Beach. The photograph was taken on Ocean Avenue in front of the LaReine Casino.

This 1917 view shows the brick walk along the ocean, heading north. To the left of center is the *New Era* statue and at the far left is the Beach View Hotel. (Courtesy Bradley Beach Historical Society collection.)

Boats and a private wagon are on the beach in this 1908 view. Bathing poles can be seen, along with benches for sitting. People are seated in the comfort of the boats rather than on the hard benches on the sand. (Courtesy Bradley Beach Historical Society collection.)

The couple in the foreground of this 1908 scene apparently forgot their bathing suits but may jump in anyway. Other people, in the typical bathing attire of the day, hold on to the safety ropes. Lifeguards would not permit anyone to swim beyond the limits of the ropes. In the late 1920s, Bradley Beach instituted the practice of selling beach badges to bathers to help pay for lifeguards and daily beach maintenance. The beach was the first in the country to have this fee. (Courtesy Bradley Beach Historical Society collection.)

This 1920s view shows the Fourth Avenue pavilion and the wide boardwalk east of it. The pavilion and boardwalk and much of the beach were destroyed in the northeast storm of December 1992. (Courtesy Bradley Beach Historical Society collection.)

All summer long, double-decker buses ran along Ocean Avenue from Asbury Park south to Belmar. The top deck of the bus was always filled to capacity, thanks to the view and the cool ocean breeze. This 1930s view shows Ocean Avenue near McCabe Avenue. In the middle of the intersection is one of the Ocean Avenue light stanchions, which were very decorative but extremely hazardous to motorists turning the corners onto and off of the avenue. Rows of what are now vintage cars line both sides of the avenue. (Courtesy Bradley Beach Historical Society collection.)

The beach is crowded with people in bathing suits and beach chairs—offering at least some comfort. Also on hand in the summer of 1912 are lifesaving boats. Housing was still allowed on the east side of Ocean Avenue. (Courtesy Bradley Beach Historical Society collection.)

Mayor Frank Borden poses with his reelection committee in 1925. The major theme of his campaign was to try to get Ocean Grove to allow Ocean Avenue to be extended across Fletcher Lake into the religious community. However, the blue laws that had been in force since its inception kept Ocean Grove from wanting to be connected. No liquor was to be sold or consumed inside Ocean Grove ever, and on Sunday no vehicular traffic was allowed and the beaches and all businesses were closed. The Methodists of Ocean Grove took their religion seriously. Although Borden won reelection, he lost the fight for Ocean Avenue. (Courtesy Bradley Beach Historical Society collection.)

The three flags next to the Fifth Avenue gazebo were lowered to half-staff on September 11, 2001. The flagpoles are set in a large flower bed displaying large white letters that spell "Bradley Beach." The flower bed is planted annually with plants raised from seedlings in the bourough's greenhouse. Colorful flowers from the greenhouse nursery are planted all around the borough. (Courtesy Bradley Beach Historical Society collection.)

Fishermen and their boats are photographed on the Newark Avenue beach in the 1930s. In 1898, William Larrabee and W.T. Gisson started a fish market on the corner of Newark and Central Avenues. The store was destroyed by fire in 1902 and, the following year, John Woolley bought the business and started fishing again. (Courtesy Bradley Beach Historical Society collection.)

Fishermen display their day's catch, and people on the beach bought the fish from them, fresh off the boats. The balance of the catch was taken to the market on Newark Avenue. (Courtesy Bradley Beach Historical Society collection.)

Horses supplied the power necessary to pull the boats to the water and then haul them out of the water at the end of the fishing day. A tunnel under the boardwalk allowed the fish wagons to get to Woolley's Newark Avenue fish market. (Courtesy Bradley Beach Historical Society collection.)

The fishermen, many of them mostly Norwegian, get their boats ready to be pulled to the water by the horse. A dog supervises. At the fishery, the men have use of a bunkhouse and kitchen. Across from the market is a wide lot where they spread their nets to dry. In stormy weather, the men mend the nets on a shuttle in the huge equipment barn. (Courtesy Bradley Beach Historical Society collection.)

After hauling the boat from the water, the horses pull the wagon loaded with baskets of fresh fish to Woolley's Market. The fishery is a community in itself. In addition to the market, there are the packing house, stable, equipment barn, and offices. (Courtesy Bradley Beach Historical Society collection.)

The birds are hungry and want to eat the fresh fish in the boat. Some of the fish struggle so much in the net that they hurl themselves overboard, either into the water or onto the sand. Then the birds get their meal. When the fish arrives at the market, it is sorted and boxed whole in ice and shipped to New York, St. Louis, and Chicago. (Courtesy Bradley Beach Historical Society collection.)

The public library's float takes part in the 1998 Memorial Day parade. (Courtesy Bradley Beach Historical Society collection.)

The 1999 Memorial Day parade down Ocean Avenue includes the annual contingent of the Benny Brigade, visitors who spend their summers at Bradley Beach. The Bennys carry beach chairs, which they snap to the beat of the music played on a boom box. They are always a crowd pleaser. The term Benny came from the railroad baggage handlers, who labeled the luggage BNENY, standing for Bayonne, Newark, Elizabeth, and New York. Soon, the passengers were also called Bennys and the nickname stuck. (Courtesy Bradley Beach Historical Society collection.)

The LaReine Hotel, known for elegance and hospitality, and its adjoining neighbor are seen from the air in this 1960s view. In front of the two hotels is the dolphin statue and fountain. (Courtesy Bradley Beach Historical Society collection.)

The neighbor of the LaReine is the Hotel Ritter-Grossman. This 1930s promotional card offers special Decoration Day (Memorial Day) weekend rates of $5 per day, seasonal rates from as low as $25 per week including all meals, tennis courts, a swimming pool, and beach activities. (Courtesy Bradley Beach Historical Society collection.)

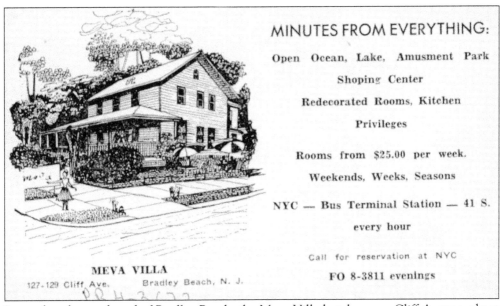

Located at the north end of Bradley Beach, the Meva Villa hotel was on Cliff Avenue, about one block from the ocean. The 1930s advertisement offers rooms from $25 per week, which at the time must have been a standard price for the summer. (Courtesy Bradley Beach Historical Society collection.)

The Sea Cliff Hotel, on McCabe Avenue, was large and close to the ocean. This view was taken in the 1920s. (Courtesy Bradley Beach Historical Society collection.)

The Hotel Alpine stood one block west of the Sea Cliff Hotel. The awnings on the big porch must have provided welcomed relief from the afternoon sun. (Courtesy Bradley Beach Historical Society collection.)

The Jewish War Veterans memorial plaque, made from part of the dolphin fountain, was dedicated in 1968 in front of the LaReine Hotel . (Courtesy Bradley Beach Historical Society collection.)

The Fourth of July parade was an annual event, featuring fire department and first aid squad equipment. This one progresses along Ocean Avenue past the LaReine and Bradley Hotels in 1970. Later, when night fell, fireworks lit up the sky.

An annual Easter egg hunt is held on the beach in front of the LaReine Hotel in 1968. Prizes ranged from Easter baskets to U.S. Savings Bonds. (Courtesy Bradley Beach Historical Society collection.)

Really getting into the spirit of the hunt, children compete for prizes, with a little help from parents and other grownups. (Courtesy Bradley Beach Historical Society collection.)

Summer visitors Mrs. W.W. Robbins and Wanda Barry of Trenton enjoy the LaReine Avenue pool at the ocean in 1927. (Courtesy Bradley Beach Historical Society collection.)

Instructor Jim Cavanaugh, track coach at St. Benedict's during the school year, gives swimming instructions in the summer of 1927. (Courtesy Bradley Beach Historical Society collection.)

Two bridges spanned Fletcher Lake between Ocean Grove and Bradley Beach: the one shown in this 1914 view of the Kent family house and another on Central Avenue, just west of this view. The Central Avenue bridge still exists and has been rebuilt several times, the latest being after the 1992 northeast storm that caused extensive damage to the shore area. (Courtesy Bradley Beach Historical Society collection.)

Looking north, this 1920s picture shows the Central Avenue bridge and the walk along the lake. In the 1950s, the walkway was removed so that Lake Terrace could be widened to allow motor traffic. (Courtesy Bradley Beach Historical Society collection.)

This 1940s aerial view of the north end of Bradley Beach shows Fletcher Lake (before the drive was built) and the Atlantic Ocean. The beaches were wide and full of bathers. On the beach to the right of the jetty is the Newark Avenue Pavilion, where public dances were held on weekends (see Bruce Edward Hall's description, page 73). Across Ocean Avenue from the pavilion is the bingo hall. One block north and one block west on Cliff Avenue is the Cliff Villa, the big house with a vacant lot next door. On the northernmost point of Bradley Beach is the Hotel Lakensea. (Courtesy Ayres private collection.)

Trimmed in patriotic bunting, the Fifth Avenue gazebo reflects the spirit of the community. With the Atlantic Ocean as its eastern border, the town lures countless visitors who mingle with residents and help keep the economy healthy. Just over 100 years ago, cows roamed along the beach, where there is now a unique tile walk and colorful flower beds, and pine forests grew where private homes and businesses stand today. Later, it was mainly the grand hotels that provided summer visitors with comfort and ocean breezes. In current times, the restaurants, movie theater, and other businesses offer entertainment year-round. Bradley Beach is no longer just a summer resort but a self-sustaining community that welcomes visitors throughout the year.

BIBLIOGRAPHY

Cottrell, Richard F. *Neptune City Millennium History*, TFH Publications, Neptune City, New Jersey, 2000.

Crawford, Gary S. *The Trains Used to Run through Here*, unpublished manuscript.

Eid, Joseph. *Trolleys in the Coast Cities*, privately published, Brick, New Jersey, 1979.

Hall, Bruce Edward. *Tea That Burns*, pages 240–244, The Free Press, New York, 1998.

Lewis, Evelyn Stryker. *Neptune and Shark River Hills*, Arcadia Publishing, Charleston, South Carolina, 1998.

Salter, Edwin. *A History of Monmouth and Ocean Counties*, Gardner & Son, Bayonne, New Jersey, 1890.

Travelers Official Railway Guide, National Railways Publication Company, New York, June 1893 and March 1964.

White, Robert L. *A Compilation of New Jersey Railroad History 1877-1887*, privately published, Manasquan, New Jersey, 1996.

Wilson, Harold F. *The Jersey Shore*, Vol. I, Lewis Historical Publishing, New York, 1953.

Wood, Don, Tom Gallo and Joel Rosenbaum. *The Unique New York and Long Branch Railroad*, Audio-Visual Designs, Earlton, New York, 1985.